PLAY KIND

Acts of Kindness for Kids

By: Jacquelyn Stagg Illustration: Katerina Kalinichenko

Published and written by Jacquelyn Stagg
Illustrations by Katerina Kalinichenko
Edited by Darcy Werkman

ISBN: 978-1-7751833-6-5

www.jacquelynstagg.com

Dedicated to my girls.
May you always choose kindness.

ACTS OF KINDNESS

1 LEMONADE FOR A GOOD CAUSE

Beat the heat and add a twist of kindness to this classic activity!

Running a lemonade stand is not only a great way to learn about business and the value of money, but it can also be a great way to show kindness!

Think about donating all or a portion of your profits to a charity that is important to you.

SUPPLY LIST

- ☐ Table/Stand
- ☐ Sign
- ☐ Tape
- ☐ Cups
- ☐ Pitcher
- ☐ Lemonade
- ☐ Ice Cubes
- ☐ Donation Jar

*All **Play KIND** activities require adult supervision. Use good judgment when setting up activities.*

 #PlayKindKids | Share your experience on social media to help encourage others to *Play KIND* too!

2 PACK A BACKPACK

Get in the school spirit by picking up a few extra back-to-school supplies this year and help a student in need!

Not all families can afford the supplies needed for their child to begin school. Packing a backpack is a simple way that you can help fill this need.

Many communities already have a backpack program in place! Contact your local school board to find out which specific supplies are needed and where they can be dropped off.

SUPPLY LIST

☐ Backpack

☐ Pencils

☐ Crayons

☐ Erasers

☐ Scissors

☐ Glue Stick

☐ Notebooks

☐ Binder

☐ Calculator

☐ Lunch Box

*All **Play KIND** activities require adult supervision. Use good judgment when setting up activities.*

#PlayKindKids | Share your experience on social media to help encourage others to *Play KIND* too!

BAKE COOKIES FOR A NEIGHBOR

Nothing says *"Welcome to the Neighborhood!"* **better than a batch of homemade cookies!**

Baking can be used as a fun way to learn invaluable life skills and educational concepts like reading, mathematics, and science!

Grab your favorite recipe and throw a little kindness into the mix by giving the cookies to your neighbors as a thoughtful gift!

SUPPLY LIST

☐ Favorite Cookie Recipe

☐ Cookie Ingredients

☐ Baking Equipment

☐ Cookie Cutter

☐ Oven

☐ Basket/Container

*All **Play KIND** activities require adult supervision. Use good judgment when setting up activities.*

#PlayKindKids | Share your experience on social media to help encourage others to *Play KIND* too!

1 POSTCARDS FOR SENIORS

Did you know that seniors typically spend most of their time alone?

Taking time out of your day to create a homemade postcard, picture, or card for a senior will brighten their day and make them feel special and cared for.

Get in touch with a local seniors' residence to arrange a time to visit or drop off your artwork.

SUPPLY LIST

☐ Paper/Cardstock

☐ Crayons

☐ Envelope

*All **Play KIND** activities require adult supervision. Use good judgment when setting up activities.*

5 BEE KIND ROCKS

This craft is perfect for a gift or a simple keepsake as a reminder to *Bee Kind!*

Gather a few rocks and your painting supplies, and let your creativity run wild with this bee-themed art project with a kind message!

Take the time to think about what it really means to be kind as you are completing this craft.

SUPPLY LIST

☐ Smooth Rocks

☐ Acrylic Paint

☐ Sealer

☐ Paint Brush

☐ Water

☐ Markers

*All **Play KIND** activities require adult supervision. Use good judgment when setting up activities.*

6 DONATE TO THE FOOD BANK

Did you know that one in seven children are currently facing hunger in America?

You can be part of the solution to help ensure that every child has access to the food that they need by simply donating to a food bank.

Contact your local food bank to learn about which foods are needed and other practical ways that you can help.

SUPPLY LIST

☐ Canned Beans

☐ Canned Vegetables

☐ Canned Fruits

☐ Canned Meat

☐ Packaged Grains

☐ Pasta Sauce

☐ Baby Food

☐ Pet Food

☐ Donation Box

*All **Play KIND** activities require adult supervision. Use good judgment when setting up activities.*

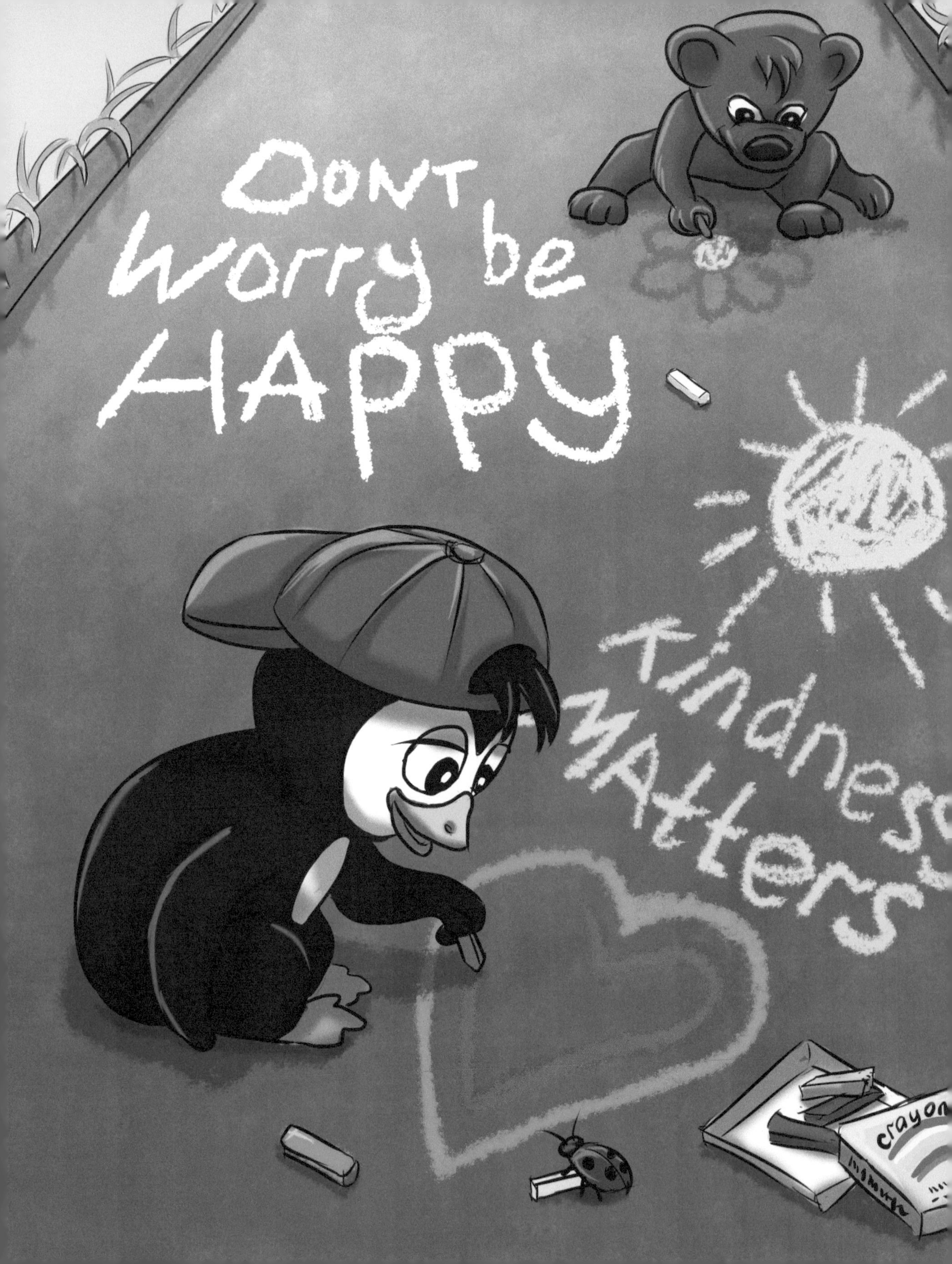
DONT
Worry be
HAPPY
Kindness
MATTers
crayon

7 SIDEWALK CHALK MESSAGES

Spread kindness with messages on the sidewalk for people passing by!

Take the time to brainstorm some ideas that you could write or draw that would make someone smile.

Words of encouragement, a joke, or pictures of happiness — the options are endless for you to get creative with this kind activity!

SUPPLY LIST

☐ Sidewalk Chalk

*All **Play KIND** activities require adult supervision. Use good judgment when setting up activities.*

BUILD A BIRDHOUSE

Being kind to animals is one of the easiest ways to learn about compassion!

Building a birdhouse is not only a great way to learn some basic woodworking skills, but it will leave you with a sense of accomplishment while also providing a new home for a bird!

Paint it, place it, and practice patience while you wait for the birds to move in!

SUPPLY LIST

☐ Birdhouse Kit
  (Available at your local building store!)

☐ Glue

☐ Hammer

☐ Nails

☐ Paint

*All **Play KIND** activities require adult supervision. Use good judgment when setting up activities.*

 #PlayKindKids | Share your experience on social media to help encourage others to *Play KIND* too!

PLANT A GARDEN

Planting a garden is a fun outdoor activity that you can share with your family!

Gardening teaches responsibility, patience, and a respect for nature while you learn to care for a tiny seed by giving it everything that it needs to grow.

Try planting a pizza garden with tomatoes, peppers, and basil so that you can experience the fruit of your labor!

SUPPLY LIST

☐ Garden Seeds

☐ Flower Pots

☐ Garden Soil

☐ Watering Can

*All **Play KIND** activities require adult supervision. Use good judgment when setting up activities.*

10 DONATE UNUSED TOYS

Donating unused toys is an excellent opportunity to give to those who are less fortunate.

While it can sometimes be difficult to part ways with your toys, you can feel good about your decision knowing that they will be a gift to a child who does not have a lot of toys.

Some charities have specific guidelines for packing donations. Always check before you drop off your stuff or arrange for a pickup.

SUPPLY LIST

☐ Donation Box

*All **Play KIND** activities require adult supervision. Use good judgment when setting up activities.*

 #PlayKindKids | Share your experience on social media to help encourage others to *Play KIND* too!

11 FRIENDSHIP BRACLETS

Get nostalgic with this classic activity of making and giving friendship bracelets!

A bracelet made with love is a great way to show someone that you are thinking about them and that they are an important person in your life.

The ways to make a friendship bracelet are endless. Whether it is made with beads, fabric, or dry pasta, the message of inclusivity remains the same.

SUPPLY LIST

☐ String

☐ Beads

☐ Scissors

*All **Play KIND** activities require adult supervision. Use good judgment when setting up activities.*

12 VOLUNTEER AT A SOUP KITCHEN

Volunteering at a soup kitchen is a great way to do something as a family while helping those in need.

Many people who are struggling to make ends meet rely heavily on soup kitchens, especially during the cold winter months.

This is the perfect opportunity to give of your time and resources to help ensure that all families have access to a warm meal.

SUPPLY LIST

☐ Apron

*All **Play KIND** activities require adult supervision. Use good judgment when setting up activities.*

#PlayKindKids | Share your experience on social media to help encourage others to *Play KIND* too!

13 GARBAGE PICK-UP DAY

Nobody likes a litterbug!

While it is unfortunate that this is even a problem, there are a lot of people who still don't bother to throw away their trash responsibly. Take the time to learn about the importance of composting, recycling, and disposing of your waste appropriately.

Be sure to make safety a priority with this activity, while helping to create a clean environment for everyone to enjoy!

SUPPLY LIST

☐ Garbage Bag
☐ Gloves
☐ Shoes/Boots

*All **Play KIND** activities require adult supervision. Use good judgment when setting up activities.*

11 THANK-YOU CARD FOR MAIL CARRIER

National Mailman Day is on February 4, and it is the perfect time to thank your mailman!

Mail carriers deliver mail in all weather conditions, and if they are on a walking route, they may walk over ten miles every day delivering mail!

A simple thank-you card is a nice way to let them know you appreciate everything they do.

SUPPLY LIST

☐ Paper/Cardstock

☐ Crayons

☐ Envelope

*All **Play KIND** activities require adult supervision. Use good judgment when setting up activities.*

15 WINTER COAT DRIVE

Donate a winter coat and help someone keep warm this winter!

As the weather begins to get colder, we need to be aware that not everyone has a warm place to call home.

You can start by gathering any extra or outgrown coats you may have lying around your home. To be even more helpful, you can consider reaching out to family and friends and organize a winter coat drive.

SUPPLY LIST

☐ Coat Hangers

☐ Sign

☐ Donation Box

*All **Play KIND** activities require adult supervision. Use good judgment when setting up activities.*

 #PlayKindKids | Share your experience on social media to help encourage others to *Play KIND* too!

Initiative

The **Play KIND Initiative** is a new program that we have created as a way to give back to our community, and simply help teach our daughter different and tangible ways to be kind! Together as a family, we will decide where, and how we can be the biggest help by using a portion of our previous month's profits from this book!

Do you know a child who could benefit from the Play KIND Initiative?

Please get in touch.

www.jacquelynstagg.com/playkind

A note from the Author

I would like to thank my readers from the bottom of my heart for your on-going support. Every time that you purchase a book from an independent author, an actual person *(me)* does a happy dance!

If you have enjoyed reading this book as much as I have enjoyed writing it, please consider taking a few moments to leave a quick review on ***Amazon.com***.

Stay kind,

Jacquelyn Stagg
www.jacquelynstagg.com
ⓕ ⓘ ⓥ | *@jacquelynstagg*

About the Author

A mother of two and a freelance graphic designer by trade, Jacquelyn Stagg set out to write a series of children's books on a topic near and dear to her heart. Kindness. She wholeheartedly believes that kindness is the single most powerful thing that we can teach our children.

Kindness BINGO

Use this BINGO style Kindness Game to help encourage your
child to practice simple, yet powerful acts of kindness!

FREE DOWNLOAD

www.jacquelynstagg.com/kindbingo

Lightning Source UK Ltd.
Milton Keynes UK
UKHW052331151020
371675UK00001B/1